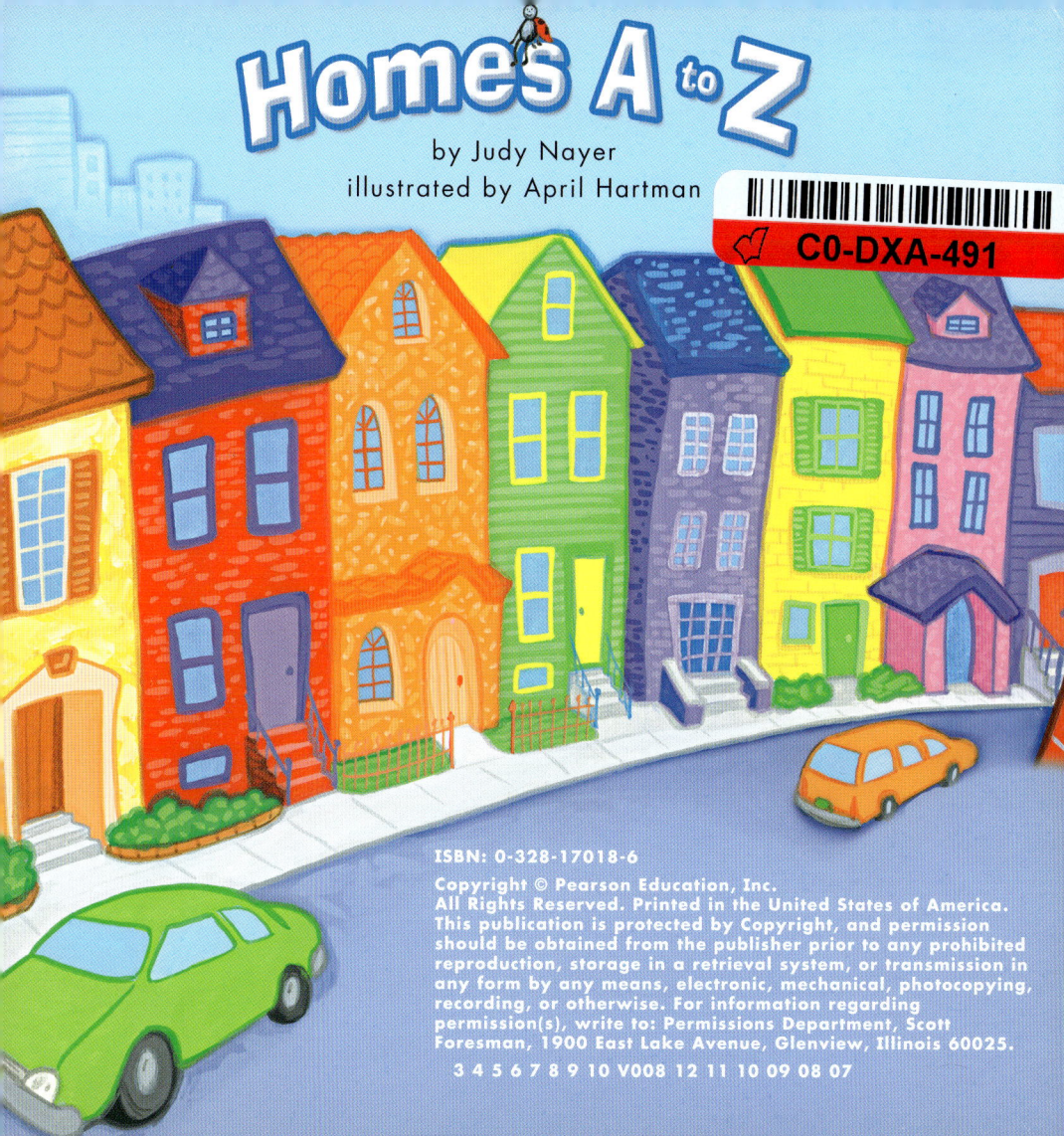

Homes A to Z

by Judy Nayer
illustrated by April Hartman

ISBN: 0-328-17018-6

Copyright © Pearson Education, Inc.
All Rights Reserved. Printed in the United States of America.
This publication is protected by Copyright, and permission
should be obtained from the publisher prior to any prohibited
reproduction, storage in a retrieval system, or transmission in
any form by any means, electronic, mechanical, photocopying,
recording, or otherwise. For information regarding
permission(s), write to: Permissions Department, Scott
Foresman, 1900 East Lake Avenue, Glenview, Illinois 60025.

3 4 5 6 7 8 9 10 V008 12 11 10 09 08 07

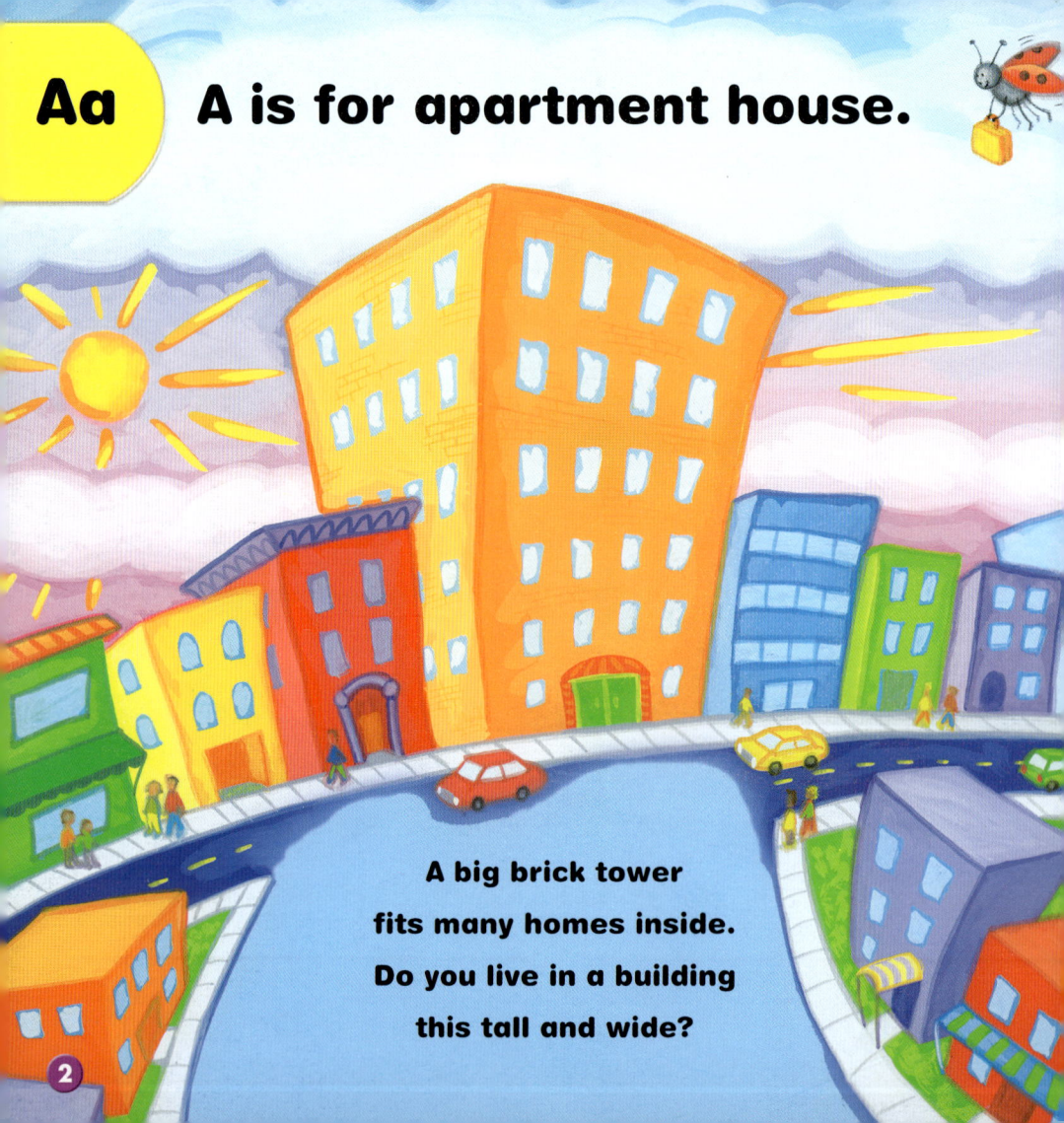

Aa A is for apartment house.

A big brick tower
fits many homes inside.
Do you live in a building
this tall and wide?

B is for boat house.

Bb

A house for a boat
keeps it out of the rain.
Have you ever seen a house
for a car or a plane?

Cc

C is for castle.

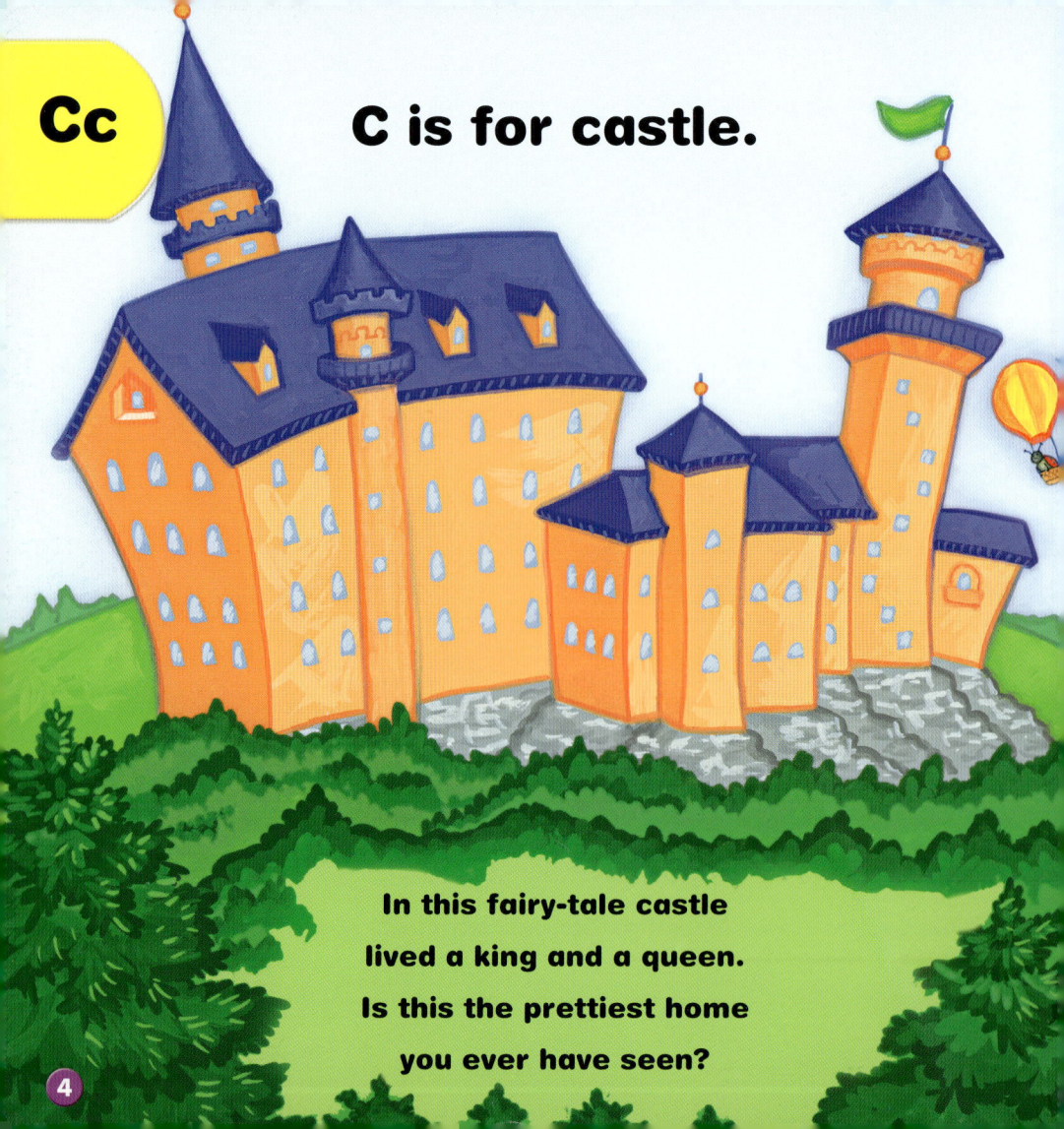

In this fairy-tale castle
lived a king and a queen.
Is this the prettiest home
you ever have seen?

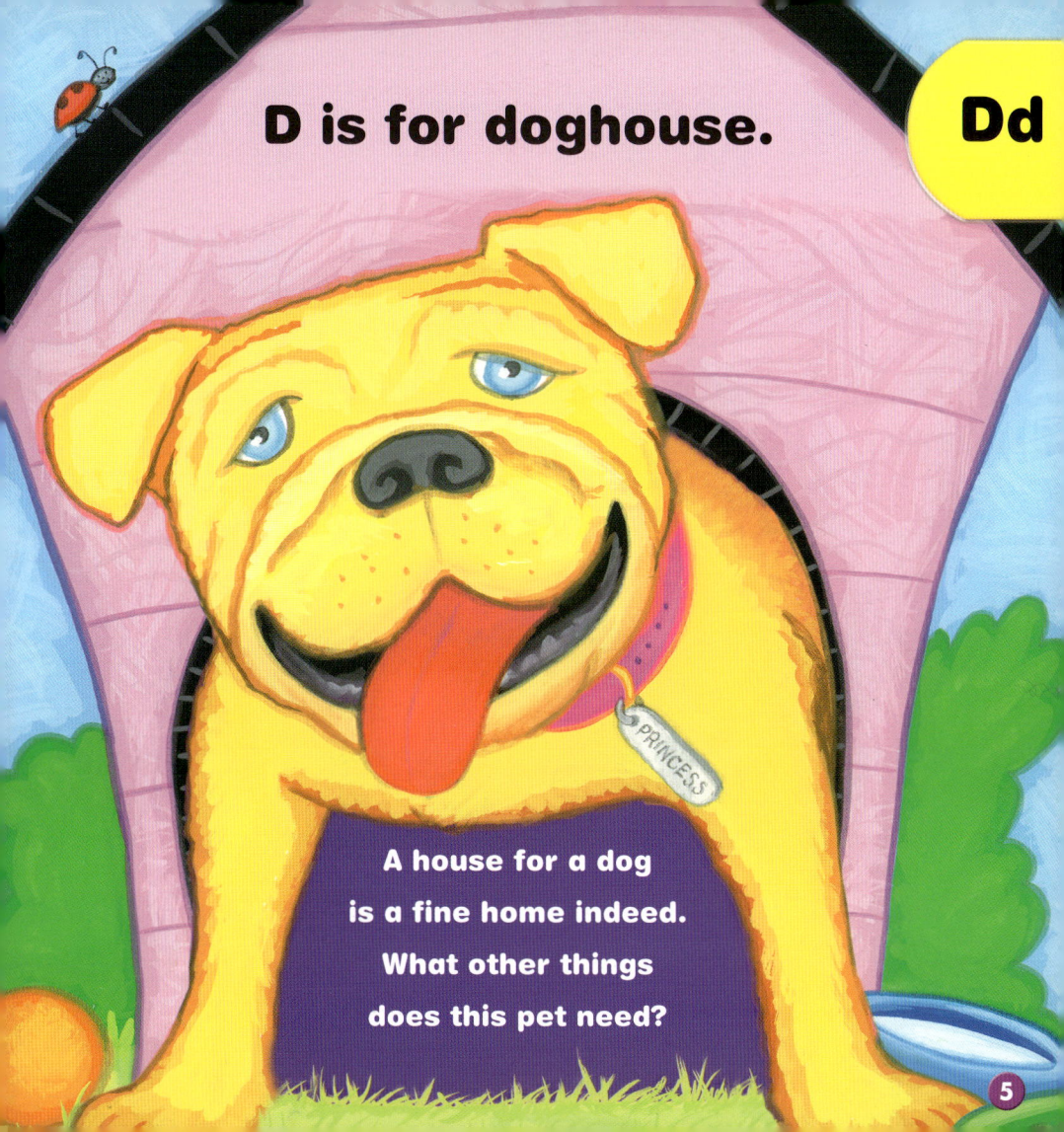

Ee

E is for earthlodge.

This native home
looks just like a mound.
What else do you know
that's big and round?

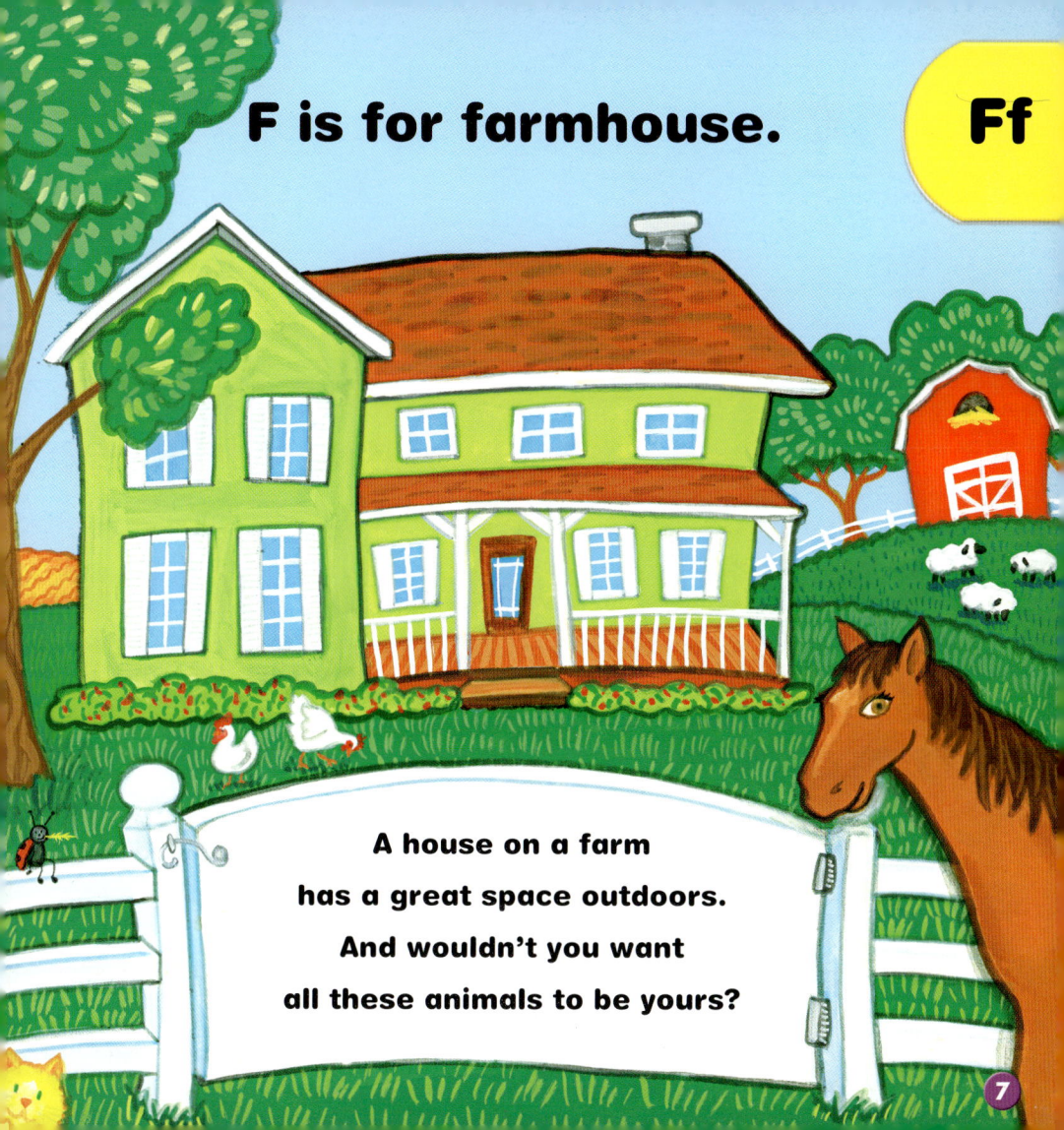

Gg

Hh

G and H are for grass hut.

A hut covered with grass is as simple as can be. What other building materials do you see?

K is for king's palace.

Kk

This palace in France
is called Versailles.
It's one of the world's biggest.
Can you see why?

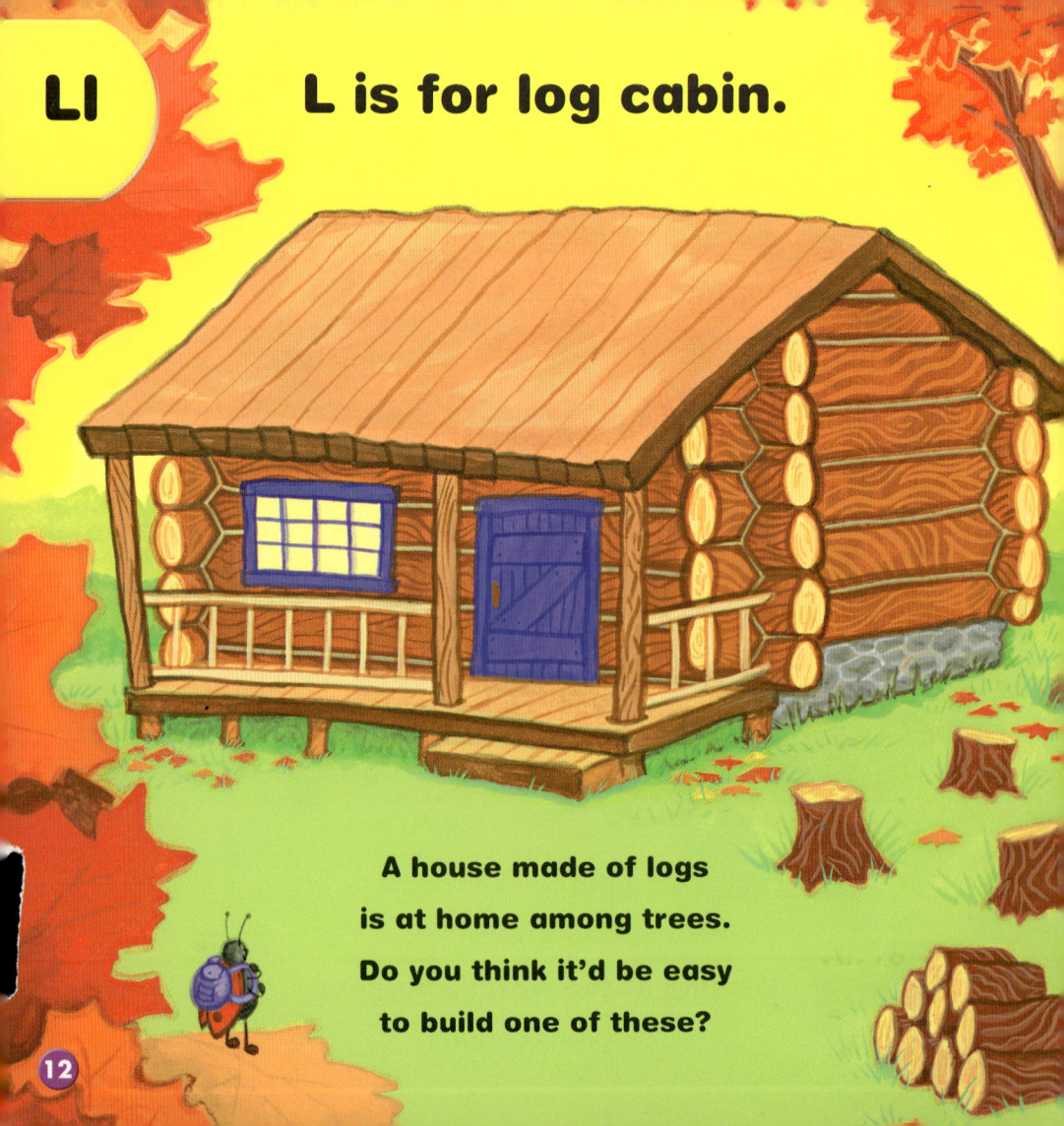

Ll

L is for log cabin.

A house made of logs
is at home among trees.
Do you think it'd be easy
to build one of these?

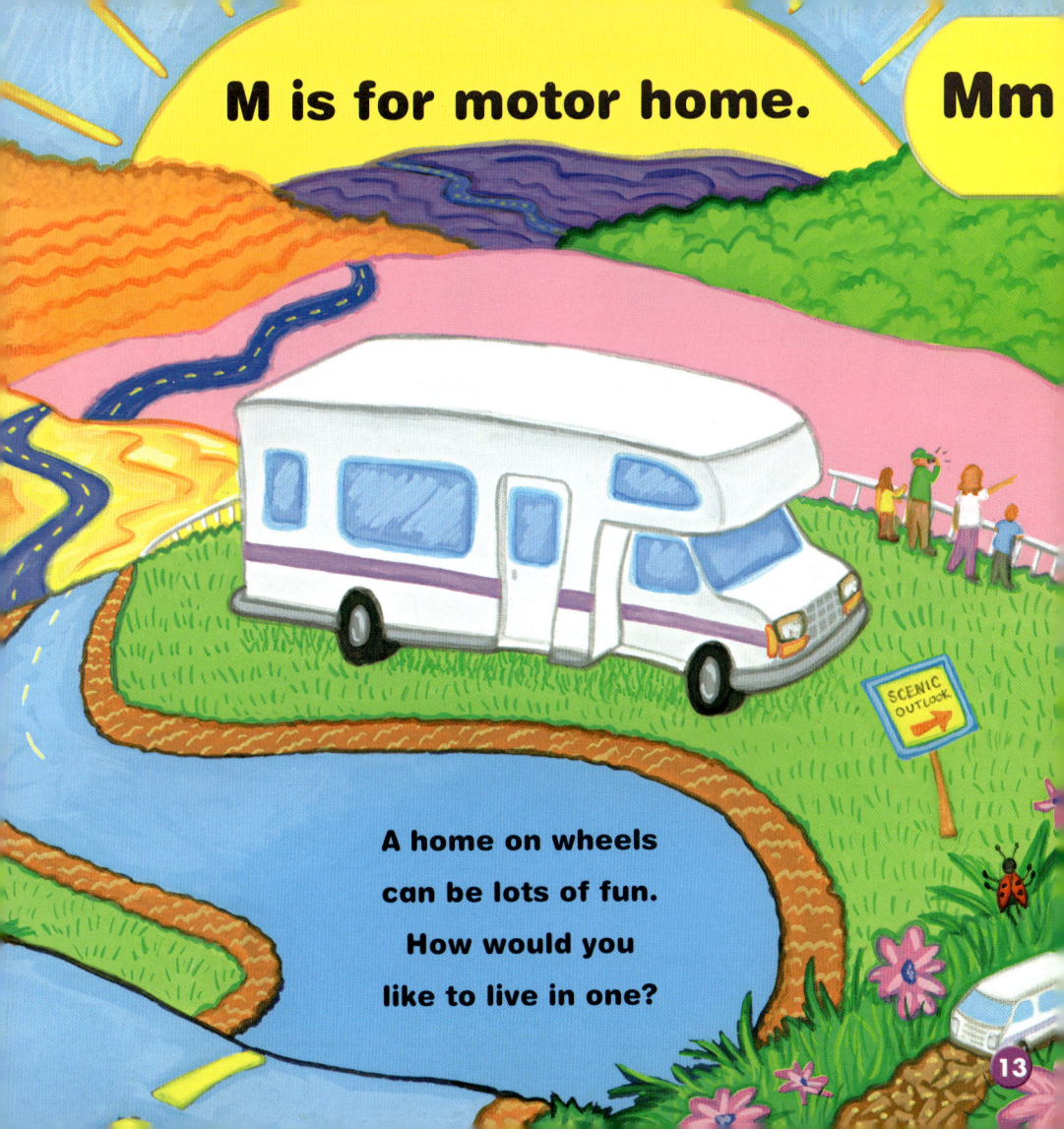

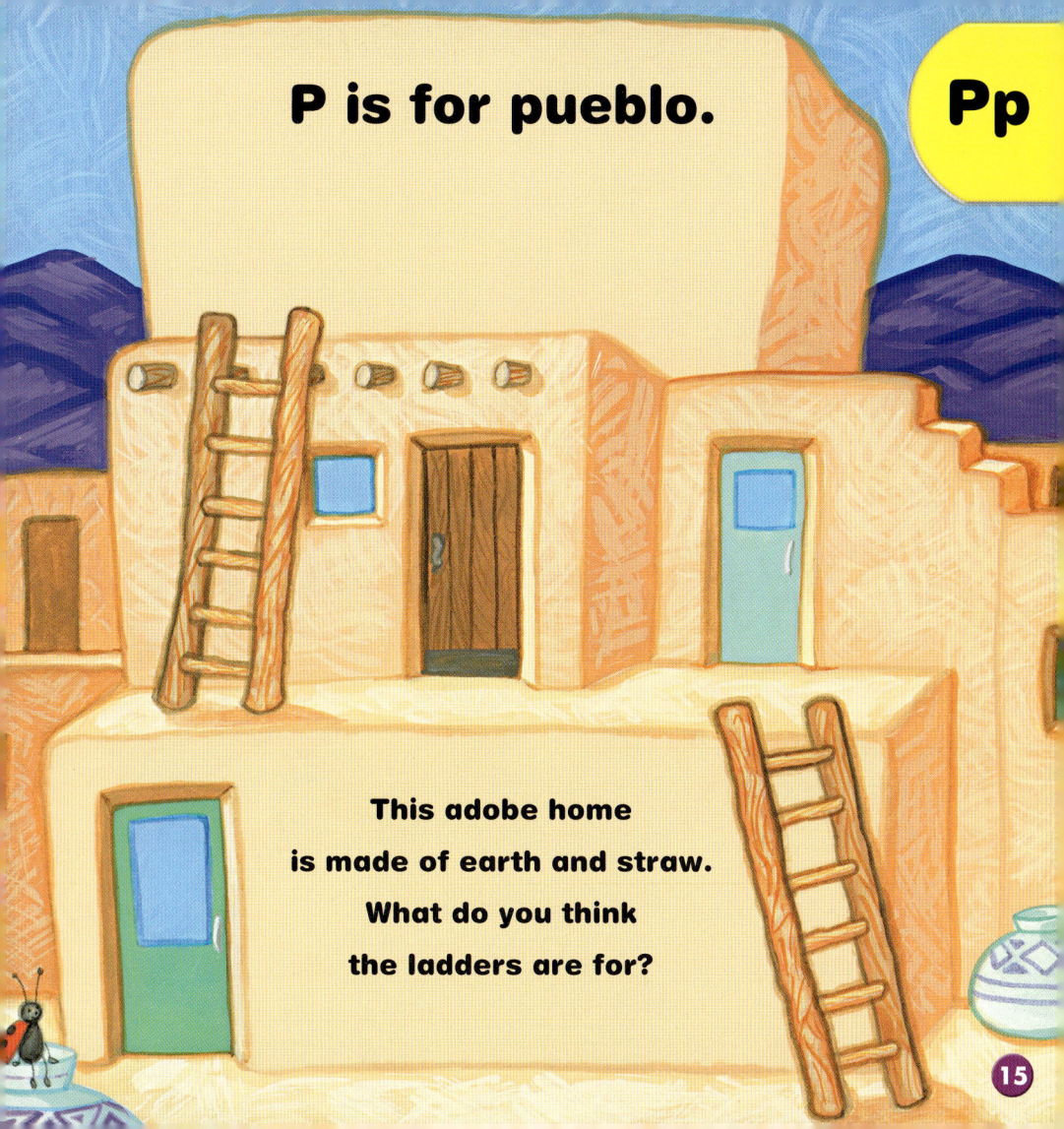

P is for pueblo.

Pp

This adobe home is made of earth and straw. What do you think the ladders are for?

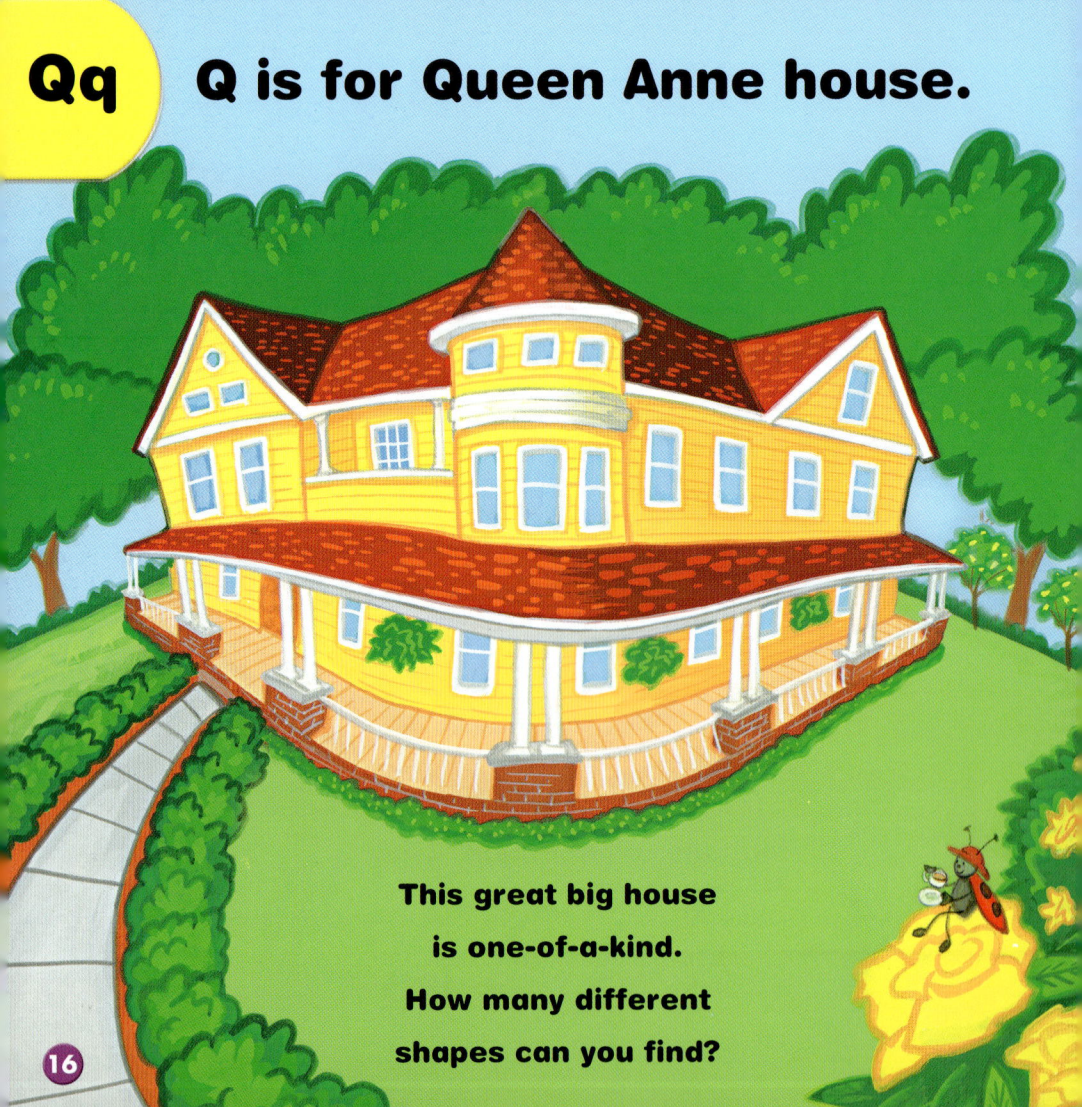

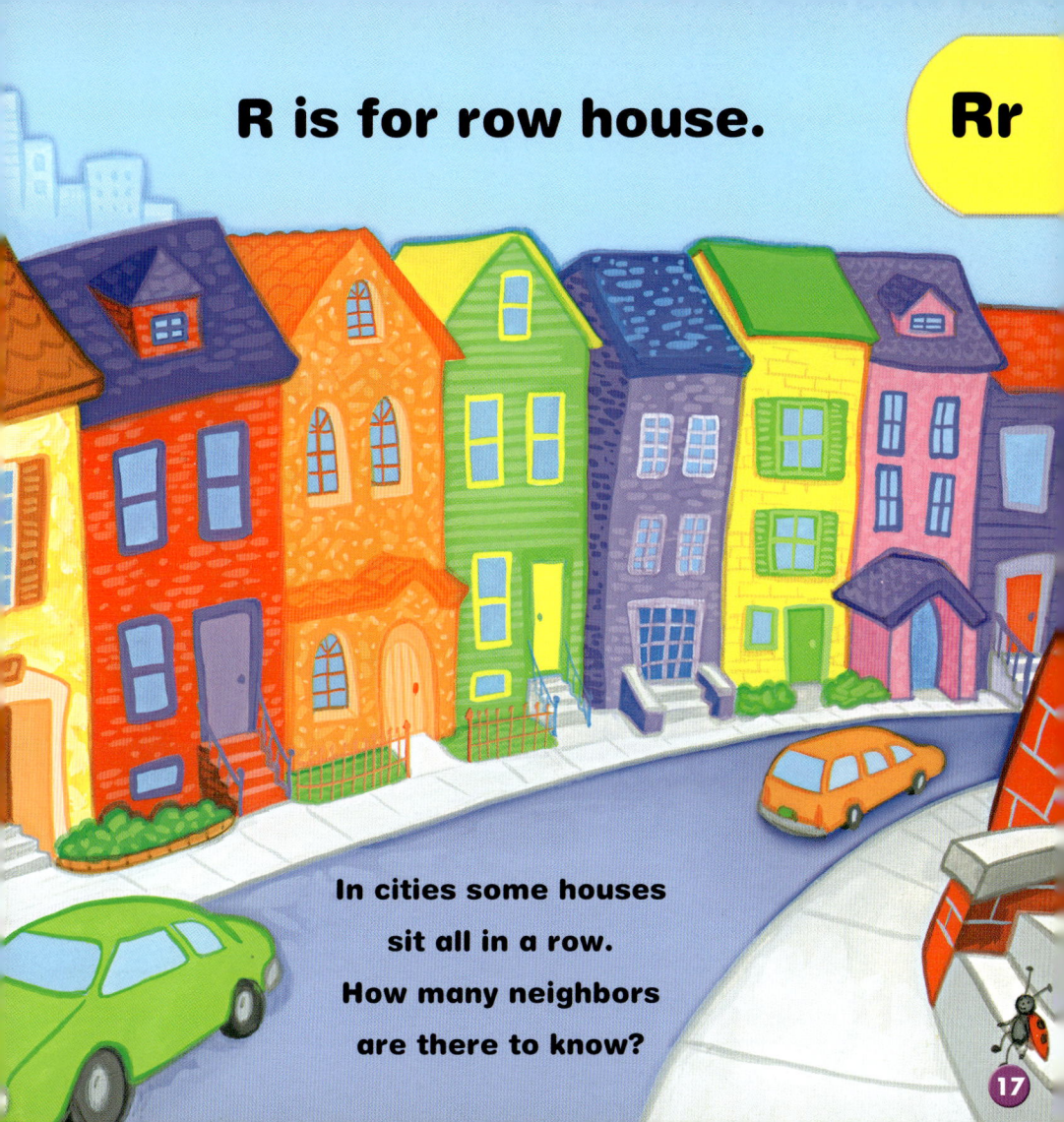

Ss

S is for stone house.

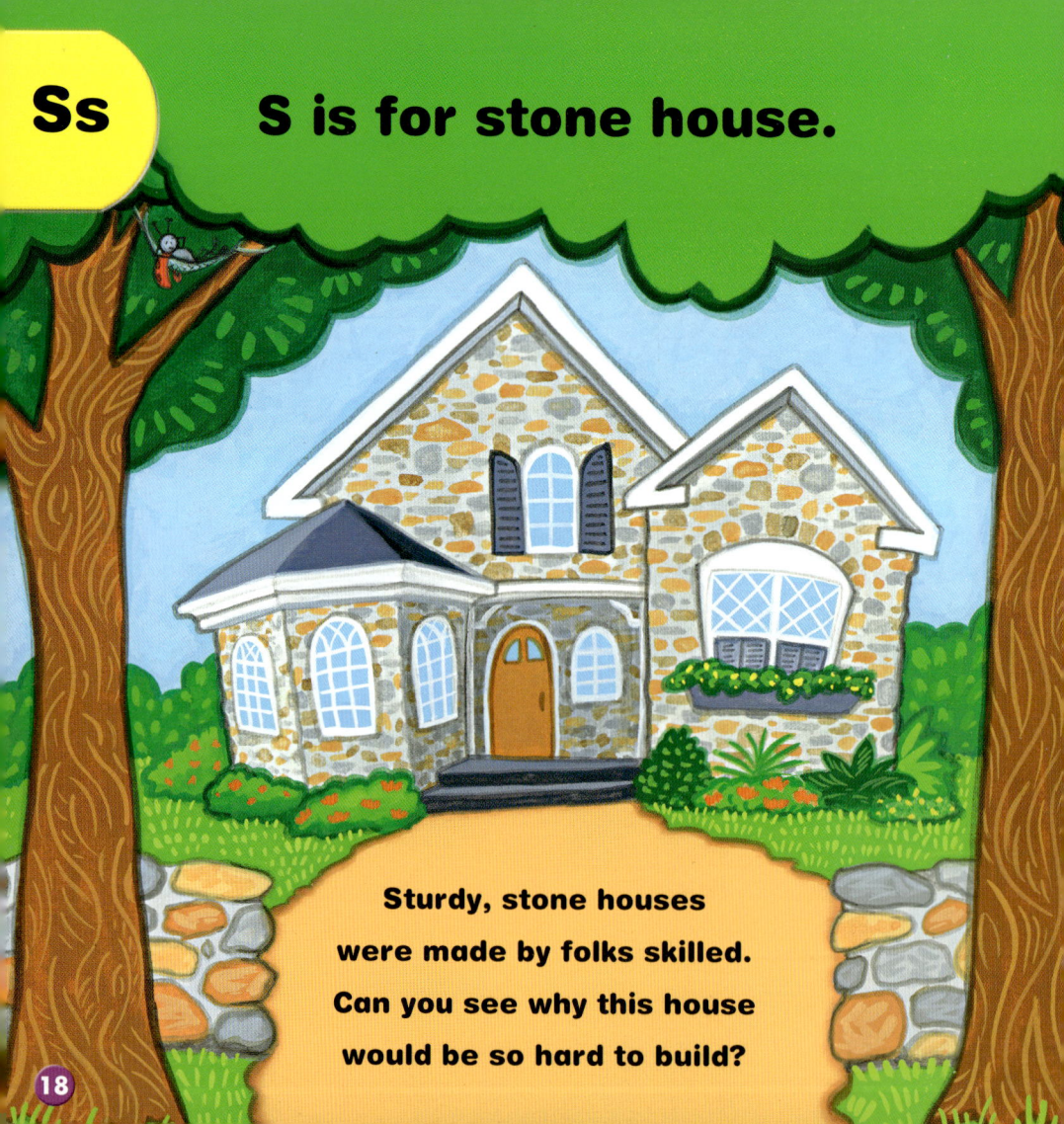

Sturdy, stone houses were made by folks skilled. Can you see why this house would be so hard to build?

T is for tepee.

Tt

**Buffalo skins
made this home long ago.
How is this tent
like the ones that you know?**

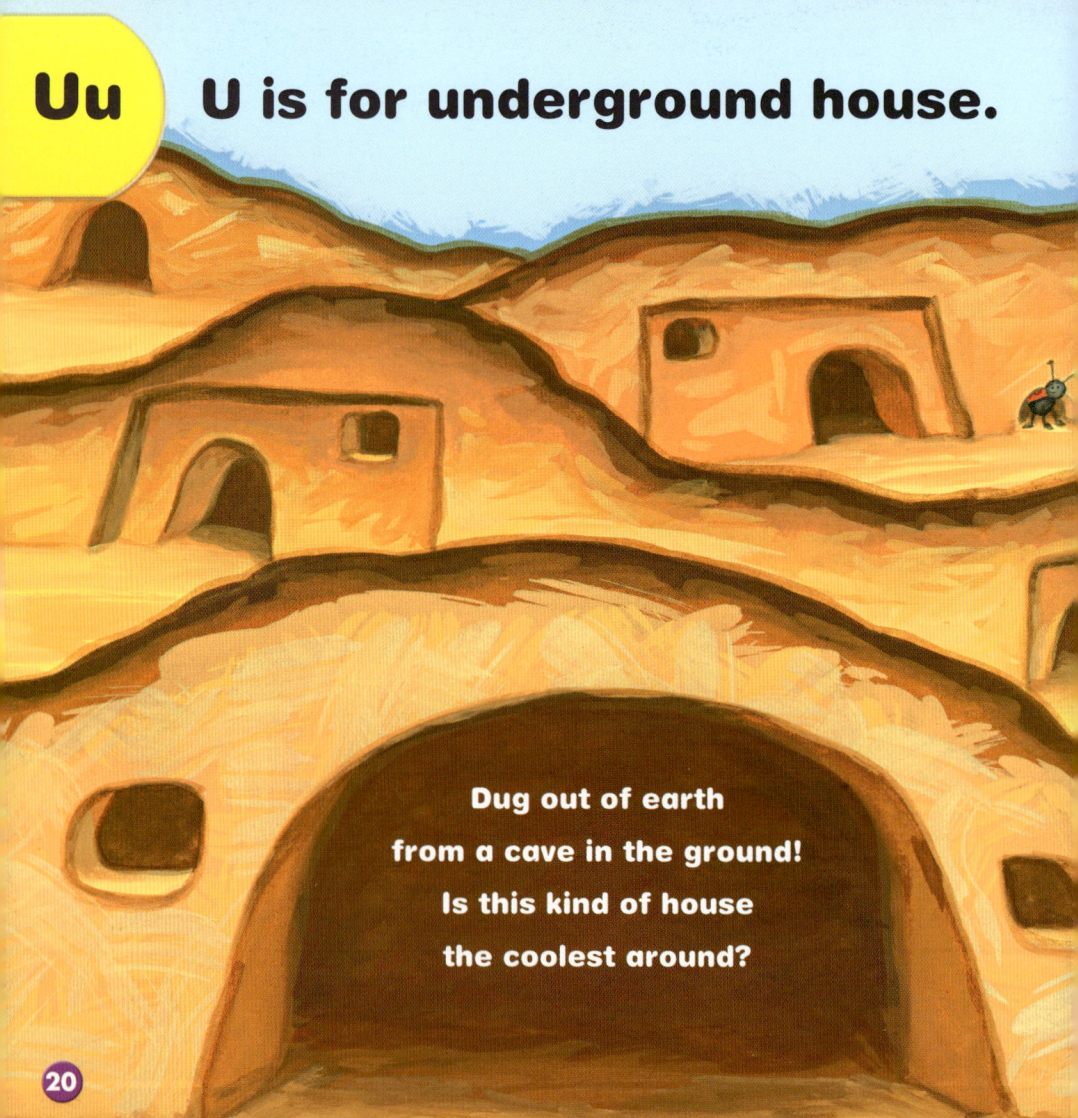

Uu U is for underground house.

Dug out of earth
from a cave in the ground!
Is this kind of house
the coolest around?

Ww
Xx

W and X are for white eXtreme house.

Perched on the shore
it faces the sun.
Is this white modern house
the type for everyone?

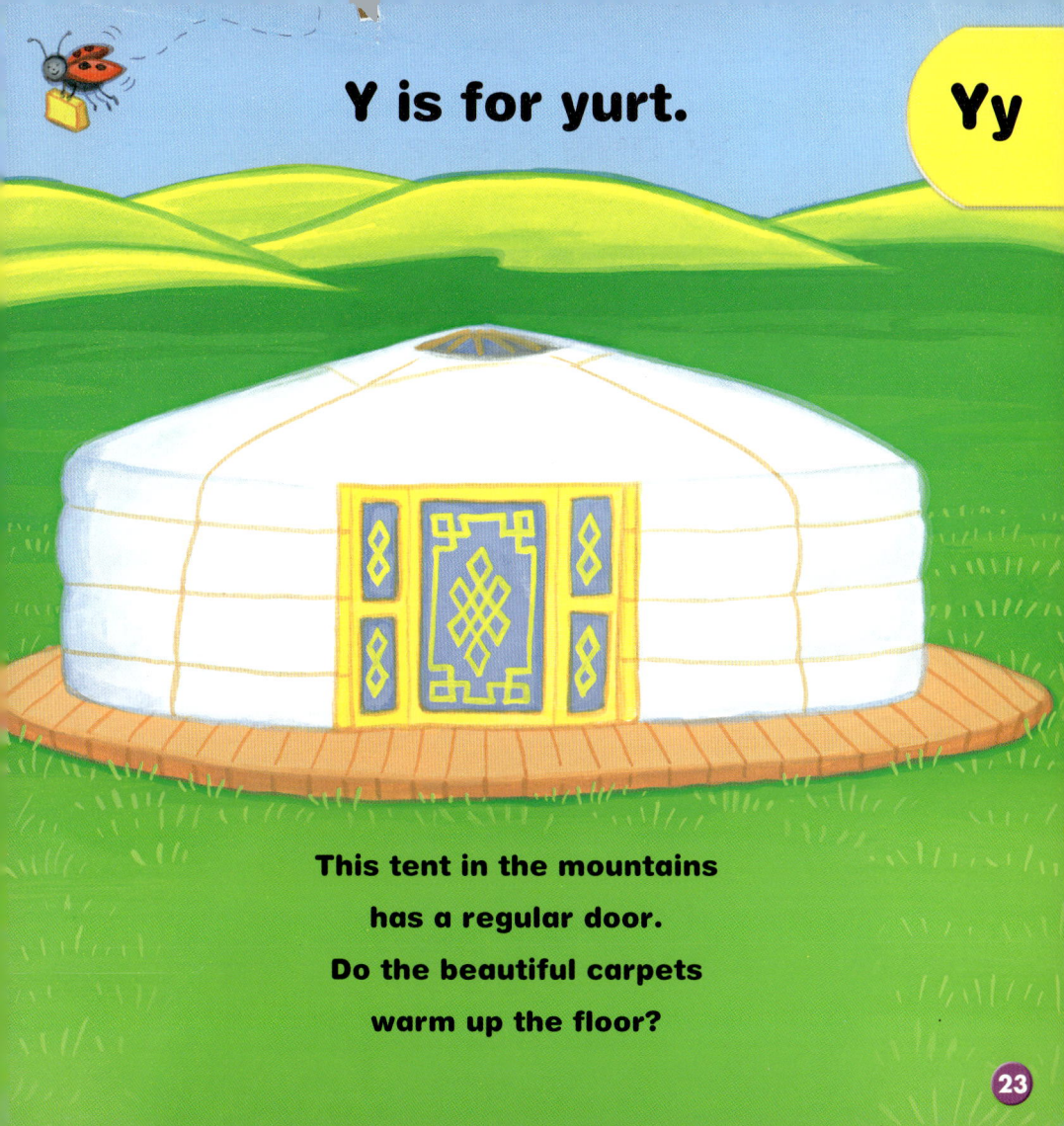

Z is for zzzzz.

Which is the home
that is perfect to keep?
The best home of all
is the one where you sleep!